True Living Sacrifice

Chaya E. Jones

A publication of

Eber & Wein Publishing

Pennsylvania

True Living Sacrifice

Library of Congress
Cataloging in Publication Data

ISBN 978-1-60880-803-8

Proudly manufactured in the United States of America by

Eber & Wein Publishing

Pennsylvania

The author wishes to thank everyone who supported her.

CONTENTS

Purity

Pure is me as my own individual person as in my mind, body, and
soul.
Pure is the pride that no one can take away from me when people
want to hold me down.
Pure is my faith in Christ as one.
Pure is the love in my heart that no one can break.
Pure is the way I carry myself with respect as for being a black fe-
male,
not in a white, or black man's world, but God's world.
Pure is standing strong for what I believe in when people try
to confuse, or mislead me to think differently.
Pure is my curly, perm hair as in nappy that descended from
the african roots of my ancestors.
Pure is my soul that is so clean, and not like any other.
Pure is being able to survive in a world full of hatred, poverty, and
violence.
Pure is an image all to itself it tells who you really are.
Pure is a goal to accomplish when you have, and other's haven't,
or even if you haven't you are determined.
Pure as rain when we cry, pure as stone when we fall, pure as in
doves when we fall in love.
Pure as in when we done wrong to others, and were forgiven.
Pure as in a leather jacket that is to say we aren't worthy when
we have a lot, and others don't have as much.
Pure is like the many crystals in a diamond that cannot
be accounted for the many lives that have been taken.

Poetry in Motion

Pen, or pencil write away on a white canvas of love.
No lies of heartbreak, and deceit.
Feeling free to express, and be one's self is truly
a blessing.
Educate the people about the writer who uses the
pen or pencil to accomplish a dream.
The sound of the african drums that beats this
amazing tune of grace.

Love in Many Forms

The red blotch is love surrounded by blackness trying to escape
and touch the white parts of beauty, and happiness.
An image of art, essence, and intelligence betrayed by a
bitter and poison love, but everyone will see the red blotch
of love overcome with a new pastel of love and color on a new
canvas of romance.

A Walk in the Moonlight

As they held hands,
and walked on the beach
talking to each other. Then
staring into one another's
eyes beaming completely
lost he pulled her close to
his side. As they kiss
they experience something so
exciting, and romantic.
Something they had never
experienced before.

The Lord's Blessing Me

Lord who gave me eyes to only see you as my Lord and Savior
not to be played with, or taken advantage of.

A mouth to speak, and share your word with others so that they
may know or want to know you.

A voice to sing your praise, not only to glorify your name, but to
comfort, and remind myself, and others, that you are greater than
life itself. Just by having you eternal life is promise, and you
went through much greater pain when you died on the cross for
my sins, and theirs, and rose from the dead.

Ears to listen, and hear your word so that it may be of some good
to me.

A heart to love, and sometimes it will end up broken, but I know
you will mend it back together in time to show how great your
love is so that I may love you, myself, and other people.

A mind of my own to be able to think for myself as of making
the right, and wrong decisions, and of you.

A body of flesh which is only temporary for now unless other-
wise by you, because when I die my body will deteriorate becom-
ing dirt from which you made me back to the ground to replenish
the earth so new seeds can form when plow, and sow properly,
but my spirit lives on forever in you.

Hands for praying, to lend a helping hand, to get a grasp of
things, maybe to heal, but only if it is in you that I should,
and lift up a person who is feeling down, or in need.

Sturdy legs with big feet to continue to walk in your path of
righteousness. To be an individual, and not follow in the foot-
steps of a stranger.

A nose to smell, and a tongue to taste.

You gave me mind, body, and soul with all these things that I
have been blessed, I can do many, and good deeds for you.

The Weather of Love

My idea of a rainy day would be you would call me up, and invite me out to dinner for a romantic evening, but by the time you got to my doorstep I would have to let you in to change, because you are all soak and wet. Then I would let your love fall on me like all those raindrops fell on you.

A warm, sunny day would be me, and you chillin' on the beach sharing an ice cream cone topped with fudge. We have a glass of ice tea to kill the thirst of our dry lips. The hot sun beating down on us as we rub sun tan lotion all over each other's body massaging one another gently with both hands. Night falls when we make love until sunset.

My idea of a snowy day would be me, and you lying in bed cuddled up next to each other playing footsies under the cover. You in your boxers, and me in my sexy, red, lace lingerie sipping on a cup of hot chocolate. After dinner, we make nonstop passionate love next to the fireplace.

Sounds of Nature

The rustling of the trees as they sway back and forth from dusk until dawn.

The chirping of a baby bird as he cries out to his mother.

The beautiful, bright, colorful leaves trampled across the steep, rocky path as hikers are going on their voyage.

The hyena's long, sharp fangs thrust savagely into it's prey.

The eagle's annoying call to warn the other animals of the dangers that await.

Even though you cannot see it, it does not mean it is not there, but I know, because I can hear the quiet sounds of the forest all around me when I am quiet, and calm.

I Love You

I love you, because you are the only one for me.
I am in love with the kind of person you are,
and not just your looks.
I love spending quality time with you.
I love to see a smile, and not a frown.
I love it when you cook a meal.
I love it when you say *I love you*.
I love you when you make each day special.

The Beautiful Moment of Being

Capture the purity of an innocent being.
Bloodshed of the enemy.
The sacrifice for justice.
A worthy cause of freedom being sound that speaks
truth loud and proud.
One who has a righteous mind, body, and soul.
Without flaws, and no imperfections.
Everlasting life, and unconditional love.

Soul

Dream big!
Full of life.
Cry no more.
Let freedom ring!
Salvation and glory in Heaven.
God's power reigns over the world,
and the righteous will claim victory.
Journey far away to the sweet promise land where happiness
lasts forever, and wisdom speaks unconditional love in one's heart.
Run wild, and laugh in the face of the enemy.
Conquer the fortress of riches.
Believe in a higher power that is greater than a man or woman.
God is His name.
Who will accept this soul other than God?
It is God who understands the soul, a queen,
that she is even if no one else does.
God is the almighty king who has sovereign power
over all things. It was God who created the soul.
God is everything within the soul.
Mind, body, and soul is one with Him.

The Artist

The colors of love painted so elegantly on canvas.
Music notes in black writing.
The sound so pleasant and soothing
can be heard all around the world.

Fountain of Youth

Drink a sip of the cool, clear water that will leave you feeling
refreshed and young.
The fountain the size, and shape of an angel.
The color of love that is pure, and whole.

God's Blessing

God instilled a power in one that is great.
The gift of song, poetry, and dance.
Wisdom, peace, love and happiness that endures forever.
One's real identity is never portrayed as trying to be
something else.

Life

Life is what you dream of, and make of it.
It is not limited by the expectations,
and opinions of other people.
No negative people around to block you from doing what makes
you happy, and even if there are, you can conquer them with
wisdom and knowledge.
A blessing in disguise is waiting to happen for you, and other
people.

Death

Gone forever, or just for a short period of time.
Calm, and blues where there is pain will heal with love.

Sweet Chocolate

Wine and dine, this fine tune you, and me.
We make love with sweet chocolate all over.

The Call

To walk the walk, and not just talk.
To fulfill the purpose, and plan for one's life.
To be a living testimony that there is a God,
and live after death in either Heaven or hell.
What will God's last words on Judgement Day
be for you?
Only one life to live.
Heaven is better than hell.

Heart's Desire

To live a righteous life, and answer my calling.
Fulfill my purpose, and plan to get to heaven.
I want to see all of my family and friends there.
A heart of riches that is love, and not gold.
My heart's desire is to be myself no matter
what other people are saying and doing,
because their opinion means nothing.
To be a true soldier.
A real man and woman in God's armed forces.
Celebrate! Celebrate!
Life that is something worth holding on to.

Live or Die in a Land of Love and Hate

To live or die in a land of love and hate.
Where many are called, but only a few are chosen.
To live freely without limitations.
The only living witness to bare the pain, and
sorrow of a lost loved one.
Waiting for the day when the enemy will fall,
and perish in hell, and the saints will
go to heaven.
Blissful moments, every now and then.
To pass through the gates of Heaven, and
not to be tormented in hell.
The greatest gift of life is to have God.
A human in disguise, and an angel in spirit
is the righteous person.
Born a prophet to the nation of Israel.
No white or black power of a man or woman.
Only the power of the almighty God.
The beginning, and the end of time.

Love, Happiness, Prosperity, and Life

Love is eternal bliss in happiness, but a detriment to the heart
when it is missing.
Born a free soul.
A slave to the human body.
I do not want pain and grief, just what is owed to me.
The opportunity to live, and be me.
Rich or poor, is not what one has, but what one does with
what they have, is going to determine if you are going to prosper
or not, and if you are going to be successful.
Dream, and speak out loud.
No need to hide behind closed doors, and feel ashamed when God
made you just fine in his own image.
God's unconditional love will encamp around me, and protect
me in a time of war.
In Heaven I will feel, and be at peace.
No more blues and weariness.

A Star's Shine

A star, and you own it so flaunt it the right way.
Beautiful not just in the sky, but on land.
Dance graciously, and sing immaculately.
No competition will ever beat me.
Beats from a radio will play my own lyrics.
The best performances in my life are not
on stage, but the message of life and death
I preach to people.
In heaven reigns kings and queens.
Forever love are my family and
friends who support me when times are good and bad.

The Vision

Take a good look at pride, tall, and fine.
Beautiful brown eyes, black hair, and a sexy body.
Do not need a camera to capture, or achieve this look.
Intelligent with a sense of mind, body, and soul.
Captivating the hearts of everyone around the world.
Strong and confident in one's self.
Bold and courageous will fight for the righteous people.

Journey of Life

Go on this journey of life through hills and valleys
of no return.
No signs of rejection from a saved Christian.
Peace of mind, wisdom, and love to carry on.
A real soldier.
A real man and woman.
The truth shall be seen and heard.
A legacy left behind for the next generation to succeed,
and conquer the enemy.
Life in Heaven for eternity, and not in hell.

Recipe for Love

One whole kiss.
Many tender touches
all over with chocolate syrup.
A cup of tea, and a heart full of love.

Just Like Me Is Love

Tall, and intelligent with a colored heart just like me is love.
Bold and confident with a beautiful smile just like me is love.
Sweet like honey, and has class just like me is love.
Religious and not self-righteous just like me is love.
Self worth and honest being just like me is love.
Proud and faithful, not fake just like me is love.
A real friend, and unconditional love that lasts forever
just like me is love.
Will defeat the enemy at no cost just like me is love.
Prospering and a soul that is saved just like me is love.

A Heart Full of Love

Precious, sweet, heart full of love.
Fallen, but it will get back up, because life goes on.
Rise adorable heart to high limits and expectations.
Strive for the best, and be yourself.
A heart full of love is unconditional, and lives
for eternity.
Broken many times, but was forgiven for all that was not pure,
and holy.
A heart full of love forgives other people for what they have done
wrong to it, and has not broken another's heart.
A heart full of love is a jewel.
A heart full of love is a memory of the good and bad times.
A heart full of love says it lived life to it's fullest potential,
and it was well worth it.
Cherish what is holy, and pure.
A heart full of love is not jealous, or hateful, but speaks and
lives the truth.
Righteous is a heart full of love that will never perish.
A heart full of love is like Heaven. Happiness and
laughter dwells within.
God heals the sad scars of a heart full of love when broken.
God's love is like a heart full of love.
A heart full of love is spiritual, and generous.

The Truth Will Be Revealed in Time

The truth will be revealed in time.
The strong will survive, and the weak will fall apart.
The truth will be revealed in time.
The saints will go to heaven, and the sinners will go to hell.
The truth will be revealed in time.
The queen will marry an angel of the Lord, and give him
children who are a blessing, and other people
will marry each other and give offspring that is a blessing.
The truth will be revealed in time.
The righteous people will praise and worship God.
The truth will be revealed in time.
God is the holy one over the world, heaven, and hell.
Also, he is over every man and woman in
the spirit and flesh.
The truth will be revealed in time. God will reign forever, and
his prophecy will come to pass.

Imagination

Red roses blush.
White rain drops.
Blue skies gray.
Black darkness.
Clear sunny days.
Yellow moons.
Singing love songs.

Unknown

The wind whispers like the world is coming to an end when
you really do not know unless you listen carefully, or maybe,
because you're like dinosaurs who are extinct to a square as
some brainless people are to a penny unlike Tony's feet that are
big, and similar to my Uncle Joe's ears.

Poet

Young, strong, and poor.
One who struggles to be free.
Stressed, and never complete.
A venturous, bold stallion.
Scarce dreams full of fantasies.
Time ticks slow but waits for no one.
A dangerous and wandering mind.
Clean on the inside but disguised on the out.
A writer of spiritual songs and African dances.
Lives the life of a sea turtle.
An outcast within the elephant's soul.
Apparently pale, and unseen voices
can never tell, or will ever know
what it is like to be a poet.

Words in Ink

The soul entangled in many lies, confusion, and lost hope.
Some inner peace, and harmony, but grief, and pain smothers
the heart.
Breath holds back all it's sweet pleasures and desires.
Mistaken identities, and prophets of great wisdom.
Evil spirits, and destruction take over the minds of many people.
Love captures some butterflies, and gives them angel wings.
A search for truth, to define one's purpose in life, and to
fulfill solemn destiny.
Guardian angel are you listening? There are prayers waiting to
be held by your tender kisses.
Will you speak of death after, or before Judgement Day?
Play a song, sound the trumpets, or weep in despair of
forgetfulness, selfish souls, or broken and abused thoughts.
The rain poured gently on bruised and delicate flesh.
Wake up child for you cannot live your life in fairy tales,
or sit and daydream false fantasies!
Notes and tension written on sheets of burning eyes released
pounding vibes from the opposite gender.
Intellect engaged in conversations. Answer and hear a disable cry
for laughter and comfort in the blue mist of clouds scattered on
land.
Illusion felt by a whisper smells genuinely of incense covered
by gold strips embraced in the arms of lace, and expensive rib-
bons.
Trustworthy, brown pen will guide the way to the golden
gates of heaven if the path of righteousness is taken. Darkness,
and pain, will batter the impotent creatures who take
the path of loneliness and hell. They will be vulnerable without
love and happiness.
Associates, friends, and family, betrayed a trust that was deep in
an emotion of passion.
Eyes full of darkness, and unending pain.

Tears glisten from nightmares, and unspoken misery while
digesting love at it's most courageous action.
Artist's paint images of racism, and deceitfulness
rather than justice or kindness, and equality that is buried
forever.
Music touches the lives of some people.
Musicians dramatize reality staring death in the hands of broken
promises.
Visions of treasured gifts pass time within an instance.
Mothers and fathers abandon or murder their young children.
Craziness is revealed, and happiness is hidden in gray skies.
Roses dance in the blazing fire of the sun.

A Musical Waterfall

Love it flows continuously through it until the water runs dry.
Soothing music is playing in the background.
It calms everything in nature.
Music of sweet passion that we both endure quietly in our hearts and
minds.
Brown, archaic, glass bowls elegantly handcrafted from delicate
hands.
Molded clay hardened and painted with oils.
Full of patience, and thoughts derived from a kindle spirit.
A musical waterfall that teaches lessons, inspires hearts, keeps us
informed on daily news and entertains the mind.
A slow jam tonight, an emotional roller coaster ride, the blissful
mood, candlelight dinner, and rose petals on the bed.
Bright, sparkling stars fill the midnight sky.
A beautiful sunset always cast at the break of dawn while tears of joy
capture sexy eyes.
Peace in a time of pain, and heartbreak.
Butterflies take control in the heat of the moment.
Survivors in the wilderness do not give up, or give in, but work
harder, because of their great strength to accomplish a task.
An artist with an abstract imagination created this image.
The pounding of an african drum is a symbol of dignity, wisdom,
courage, pride and respect.
Self-determination, and motivation overcomes all obstacles.
The sky is blue, and white flowers bud in the summer.
Cool spas, massages, and hot oil treatments.
A musical waterfall's elegance blooms throughout each year.

Love Is

Love is beautiful, kind and sweet.
Love it has our name written all over it.
Love is game that lasts forever.
Love is our heart's desire to be free, and ourselves.
Love is patience and real, not hateful,
and an imitation of lies, and broken promises.
Love is passion burning deep from within.
Love is the creator's greatest gift of life.
Love teaches us to be generous, and thankful.
Love is happiness, because we cannot go a day without a smile.

Respect and High Standards

Fly like the blue birds.
Soar high standards, and
no low class hoodlum.
Accept you for who you are.
Stand strong, and tall with
pride and respect.
A soldier's creed, and the
enemy is defeated.

One True Love

One true love it came, and will never leave me.
I found sweet destiny when I least expected to.
It will never be forgotten, copied or duplicated over.
The story will be seen and heard everywhere.

God's Annointed One

Yeah! I won anointment and favor with God.
When I do his will I am blessed, and set free from bondage.
Look at it shine and shimmer.
Beautiful on the inside and out.
There is nothing wrong with it.

Mirror Image

Beautiful reflection of kind words,
and sweet melodies not
shattered by ghetto philosophy.
Wisdom is heard and seen.

Covenant

The covenant is a bond that will last forever.
Never to be taken for granted.
A secret place where just the two of us share
that righteous divine intervention.
What God has created is holy.

Game: Queen

Queen of all divas, see and hear the men flock to my beauty.
Style is flawless: black hair, beautiful brown lips, perfect
legs, hips and thighs.
No imitation of what I should look and be like.
No players only a real man can get with and marry me.
Just as myself, and not something else.

Prophecy

The prophet walked the earth, and preached the gospel.
Truth and law words to live and die by The Ten Commandments.
Justice will be served on judgement day.
Heaven, or hell, which one will you choose?

Wedding Day

Flowers fall before me and him of different colors, shapes, and sizes.
The smell of aromatherapy, and the taste of sweet wine.
Cake and ice cream is always a delightful treat to have.
A white dress perfect for a queen, and a black tuxedo is perfect for a king.
The sunrise beautifully displayed across the land.
We enjoy each other's company, and say our vows.
There is nothing that cannot be more special than today.

Love Only Me

Love only me with intimacy.
Love only me with all your heart.
Love only me with chocolate, strawberries, and whipped cream
for dessert.
Love only me with pancakes, bacon and eggs for breakfast.
Love only me with steak and potatoes for dinner.
Love only me for who I am, and not what I have.
Love only me forever, until and after we wed: husband and wife.
Love only me as a loyal friend and companion.
Love only me in Heaven, and not in hell.
Love only me, my family, and friends.
Love only me a gift of prosperity in God's unconditional love.
Love only me is the lesson that should be taught by everyone.

Fantasy Island

The tangled liquid is suffocating the desire of reality.
Silky love pressing my face with vines thick nocturnal.
Delicious, soft wings that gives strength to the vision.
A tease of romance leads hot while I imagine the heavy flits
thickest jungle covered in molasses while being trapped in the
mist of a sexy, dark, bulky, bald warrior that is the greatest gift
I will ever know.
Birds lost in the flames of ecstasy.
Dreams flood the earth, but never mentioned or written.
Deaf, and blind I cannot find the way.
Rose petals bow at the graceful and elegant woman where she is
treated like the beautiful queen of a lion's mouth.
An apparently unseen window.

Vision Life and Love

My forest vision tell all.
The summer is away, and these sweet monsters shine.
Picture life mad beneath delicious apple trees.
Men and women pray to God for spiritual guidance.
We play on the internet above blue skies and smooth water music.
Gorgeous hair fall under those moon pedestrians of hatred.
Natural beauty rises fiercely, and will not fall over a lost cause.
His love is a mystery that is sacred and sweet.
Garden watch him bare for me.
My urge to cry, and sleepless nights is over.

Melodies of Heaven

Sweet, genuine, whispers.
Blue clouds in the sky.
White magnificent kingdom
with golden gates.
The ocean gives water, and fresh aromatherapy lingers in the air.
Confine to happiness, and never full of sorrow.
Gospel music gently playing peacefully into our hearts while
the angels dance gloriously.
Every day the disciples pray, and worship the heavenly Father.
Awake! to beautiful sunshine and no long strenuous days of work
leaving your mind overworked and stressed.
A place where my soul can call everlasting home.

Impromptu Verse

Rights to passage.
Sounds old, but wise.
Young, and gifted.
Kings and queens of royalty.

The Church

A foundation built on faith and trust in God.
The right to choose who you want to be is a blessing.
Acceptance into the kingdom of heaven on judgement day
is golden.
Pray and worship God.
All will bow at the king's throne of grace and mercy.
Preach the gospel.
Live and be righteous. Do not lay down and die.
Sing hymns, and fellowship in the sanctuary.
Take your sacrifices to the altar, and demolish
pain if you're hurting.
The righteous will walk, and not just talk.
There is no need to follow, or keep hypocrites
and the enemy around, because your life will drown,
and be over.
Be a living testimony of God's word and truth.
Shepherd girl and boy will follow, and carry on the dream.

Broken Wing Bird

The broken wing bird flew away without a trace of love.
A silent cry that can only be healed by words of wisdom, and a
delicate touch of love.
Hear and see the broken wing bird made in God's image.
The darkness, and sadness of the broken wing bird hides in the
rays of sunshine.
God will set free the broken wing bird, and it will no longer be
broken.

What I Would Do for Love

If the love in my heart could be put into words I would write
you a poem so beautiful it would bring tears to your eyes after
you read it.
If I could, I would protect and shield you from all harm and
danger.
If I could, I would sing or write you a song that would leave
you without words after you heard it.
If I could, I would take away all the pain and misery life brings.
If I could, I would spend the rest of my life with you.
If I could, I would make your life so comfortable, and
soothing, you would not want to ever part.
If I could, I would always be there for you when you need
me the most.
If I could, I would give you love that only makes you weaken.
If I could, I would leave your mind wandering with thoughts
of me that leaves your head spinning after you have thought
too much.
If I could, I would lock your love inside my heart so that if
I ever thought I would lose you, or did, I would know that
I never lost you to begin with.
If I could, I would dream sweet fantasies of you that leaves
me thinking of you night and day.
If I could, or could not, I would be all that you ever need, and
more.

The Soul Selects Her Own Society

I am in a world where there is no one, but me. I am not near, or far away. You cannot see me unless you look hard enough. Only when you are able to open up your heart not only that, but receive me with open arms, and tell me that you are here at all times whether I know it, or not, like a guardian angel that I have nothing to worry about, because you can feel my pain, and understand what I am going through, and at any time I should happen to call on a friend, you are there in a time of need. You are a beautiful and graceful bird with strong wings to catch me when I fall. A gift sent from God. Do not follow that rocky path for it will not lead the way to my heart, but if you look deep into my eyes, you will find a sweet, kind, loving and caring spirit who is dying to come out and share the love of God with other people who are hurt, lonely, sick, depressed, or in need. My spirit has been abandon for years to come, and denying itself for far too long. I cannot share my feelings, and emotions, or show myself to other people, because they do not understand, or see the real me. While all of the time you were searching, and wandering where I could possibly be. I was standing there right in front of you, and you looked right through me. Often times I try to smile, or laugh at those sweet, and most favorable memories of the past. You never saw, or felt my pain which I never wanted you to see me cry. I hope that one day you will find me. You will take the time to listen, and comfort me when I am down. When that is accomplished, sooner or later, then I will say to you, looking deep into your eyes, you have found me! You have set free a soul that had once long ago made a society of her own that she kept to herself. Then you and other people will know, and see the real me.

A Writer's Significant Other

The pen, or pencil
scribbles one, two, three…
words at a slow pace, when time
is very precious, sacred, and generous.
It laughs, cries, dances and flies
with the wind.
A religious book of spiritual hymns and parables
with morals, values, and cultural norms.
The handsome, sympathetic polar bear has
a peculiar eye.
The pen, or pencil is the writer's faithful groom to be.
The drama king in a humorous comedy sitcom.
The writer's friend, sorrow, companion and magician.
An actor of love, story teller, the song writer, and
an alternative cd featuring rhythm and blues, jazz,
pop, soul, rock and roll, rap, and gospel music.
The dove is a blessing of dreams that came true.
The love, and light of the writer's heart.
Full of life, and very energetic.
The pen, or pencil, along with it's friend, the paper,
will make the writer happy and rich.

Love Without Wisdom

The soul listens closely while the heart beats rapidly.
Full of anxiety, but the promise of love has not yet found me.
A disguise in pain. Will it ever fulfill its destiny?
God's gift is life and not death.
The writer leaves the vacant building with money, and respect,
but gains knowledge, and has inner peace within the mind and
body, after stumbling into no man's land of wisdom where peace
and prosperity intervenes all evil and destruction.
Fellow citizens who know and speak of me will always acknowl-
edge and respect me.
The people who are decent and honest will say I am a good
person.
The people who hate and slander me, will fall, and are deceived,
because they can only talk about what they think they know when
my real identity
cannot be defined in spirit or flesh, but these words of wisdom
that many people will find it hard to believe, and trust, because
they have no faith, and trust in me.
Ignorance will capture all my enemies, and intelligence will
strengthen the people who support me.
The people who have respect for me will get respect just by call-
ing me by my name, acknowledge me for who I am, and then
learn the lesson that I have taught, that is to be kind to every one.
These envious criminals want to torture me, because I am differ-
ent, and I am not going to try and fit in. I got famous, because
people cannot stop talking about me, so I will not get mad or fall
apart.
Beauty defines me, both on the inside and out.
There is love without wisdom why I do not know nor, am I going
to try to explain pity, and worthlessness of the enemy it is a waste
of my time, and effort. To think highly, or unlikely of me is a
good thing, because to set your mind in my direction, or do bodi-

ly harm is to want to be like me. Anything negative that comes my way will fall at my throne, and become positive.

Wisdom, and love, find it and tell all your friends about me. Do not mistake me for pain only but for pleasure, because nothing can stand in my way of being the one person who is decent and honest.

Confidence, dignity, and prosperity prevails upon me so go, and get yours instead of daydreaming about it, and hate on me.

Prophet

The call, the answer not lust, but there is temptation.
To preach the gospel, and send a message to people that God's
unconditional love is real, and they should praise, and worship him.
God is in the midst of my trials, and tribulations, and he will fight
my battles, and defeat the enemy.
A prophet will live and die by The Ten Commandments,
and a worthy cause.

Sex

Touch me genuine, fine looks, and a kind heart!
I will touch you back.
A man that does not have class cannot please me.
A commander in God's armed forces is my rank and recognition,
and you are a commander as well in God's armed forces.
Kiss me with your smooth and sweet lips!
I will kiss you back.
Sensual pleasure hot and tasty when we make love.
A male and female who are husband and wife is the best work of
art and sex.

Live or Die in This World

Live, or die in this world
Which one will you choose?
Part beauty, and the other half ugliness.
God made everything that is
beauty, and sin is the ugliness of this world.
Live, or die in this world.
Live a righteous life, or die a lost hope, and cause.
The writer's spirit wants to live
righteous, and be a living testimony
in this world.
To preach the gospel, and God's law
The Ten Commandments to live, and die
by is what the writer chose.
The writer's spirit will rise in the kingdom of heaven,
when the body dies, and live for eternity.
Live, or die in this world.
Leave the old pain, scars, and history behind.
Accept love, life, prosperity, and a new
beginning with God as your Savior, or die in misery.
Live, or die in this world.
The writer will leave a legacy, and not tears,
so why don't you.